PIANO • VOCAL • GUITAR

Cajun & Zydeco Classics

ISBN 0-634-03705-6

HAL•LEONARD®
CORPORATION

7777 W. BLUEMOUND RD. P.O. BOX 13819 MILWAUKEE, WI 53213

Visit Hal Leonard Online at
www.halleonard.com

Contents

AMOS MOSES

Words and Music by
JERRY REED

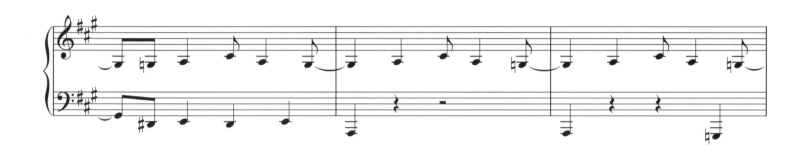

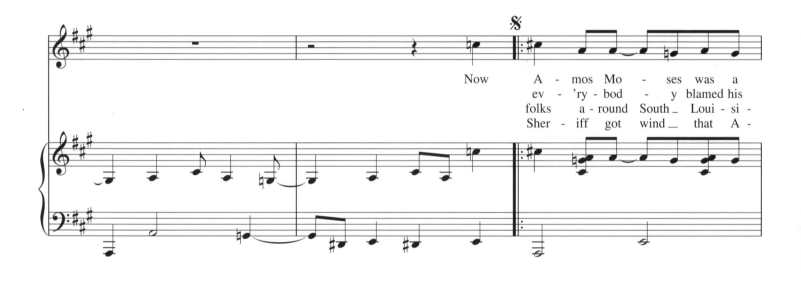

Now A - mos Mo - ses was a
ev - 'ry - bod - y blamed his
folks a - round South_ Loui - si -
Sher - iff got wind_ that A -

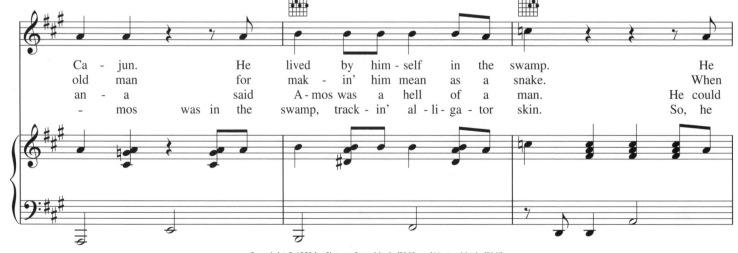

Ca - jun. He lived by him - self in the swamp. He
old man for mak - in' him mean as a snake. When
an - a said A - mos was a hell of a man. He could
- mos was in the swamp, track - in' al - li - ga - tor skin. So, he

A-bout for-ty-five min-utes south-east _____ of Thi-bo-daux, Loui-si-an-a

lived a man called Doc Mill South and his pret-ty wife Han-nah. Well, they

raised up a son that could eat up his weight in gro - ceries.

BAYOU PON PON

Words and Music by HANK WILLIAMS
and JIMMIE DAVIS

COLINDA

Words and Music by JIMMIE DAVIS,
DOC GUIDRY and L.J. LEBLANC

ché   les vieilles   femmes. ___

BIG MAMOU

Words and Music by LINK DAVIS
and MACY LELA HENRY

Moderately

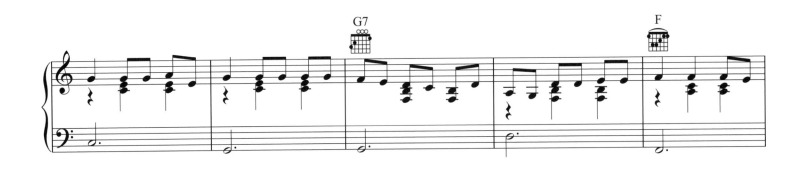

Hé, _____ mais s'en al - ler _____ à Grande Ma -

BROKEN HEARTED

Words and Music by
JOHN DELAFOSE

CRY TO ME

Words and Music by
BERT RUSSELL

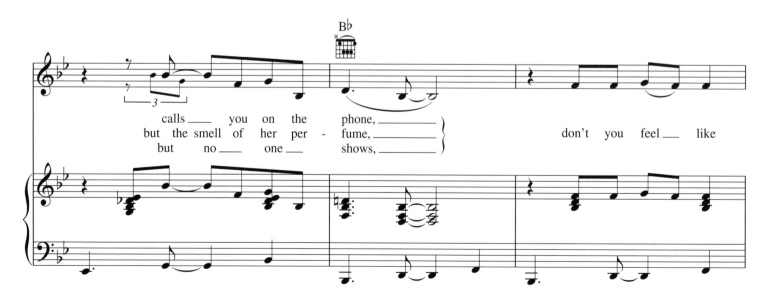

DIGGY LIGGY LO

Words and Music by
J.D. MILLER

1. *Fiddle solo*
2. *Guitar solo*

E

1, 3
A

2
A

D.S.
(with repeats)

Solo ends That's the

4

D.S. al Coda

He fin - 'lly

CODA

A

Lo.

A6

HOT TAMALE BABY

Words and Music by
CLIFTON CHENIER

I __ got a gal, ___ she's a coun - try gal. __

When it comes _ down to lov - in' me, { she knows what __ to do. ___ / she is mine, _ all mine. ___ }

You love me, hon - ey, in the morn - in', love me late at night. __

When it comes _ to lov - in' me, yeah, she's mine, _ all mine. __

HEY POCKY WAY

Written by LEO NOCENTELLI,
GEORGE PORTER, JOSEPH MODELISTE
and ARTHUR NEVILLE

Moderately fast

I'M COMING HOME

Written by CLIFTON CHENIER

I said

IKO IKO

Words and Music by ROSA LEE HAWKINS,
BARBARA ANN HAWKINS, JOAN MARIE JOHNSON, JOE JONES,
MARALYN JONES, SHARON JONES and JESSIE THOMAS

Hey now! Hey now! Hey now! Hey now!

Jock - a - mo fee na - né.__ I - ko!

See that man all dressed in green?__ I - ko, I - ko, un - day.

JAMBALAYA
(On the Bayou)

Words and Music by
HANK WILLIAMS

LOUISIANA MAN

Words and Music by
DOUG KERSHAW

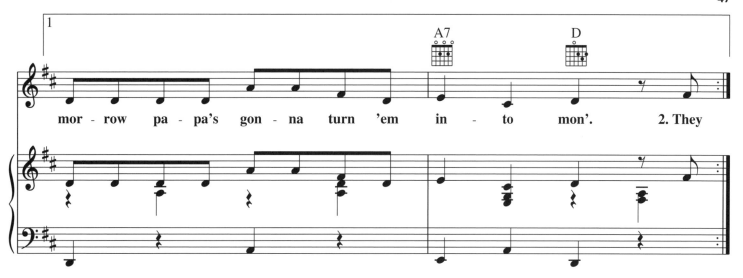

Additional Lyrics

2. They call mama Rita and my daddy Jack
Little baby brother on the floor, that's Mack.
Bren and Lin are the family twins
Big brother Ed's on the bayou, fishing.

On the river, floats papa's great big boat
That's how papa goes into town.
Takes every bit of a night and a day
To even reach a place where people stay.

I can hardly wait until tomorrow comes around
That's the day papa takes the furs to town.
Papa promised me, Ned and I could go
Even let me see a cowboy show.

I seen cowboys and Indians for the first time then
I told my papa, "I gotta go again."
Papa said, "Son, we got lines to run.
We'll come back again, first there's work to be done."

MARDI GRAS MAMBO

Words and Music by FRANKIE ADAMS,
KEN ELLIOT and LOU WELSH

Moderately

(1., 3.) Down in New Or - leans where the blues was born, __ it takes a cool cat to
(2.) In __ Gert __ Town __ where the cats all meet __ is the Mar - di Gras Mam - bo

blow a horn. __ On La - Salle __ and Ram - part Street __ the
with a beat. __ Jol - ly Chief __ was the Zu - lu king, __ and

com - bos play with a mam - bo beat. The Mar - di Gras Mam - bo,
truck on down with the mam - bo swing.

MATHILDA

Words and Music by GEORGE A. KHOURY
and HUEY THIERRY

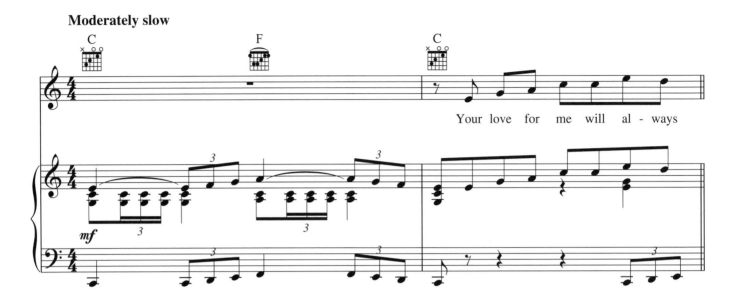

Your love for me will al - ways

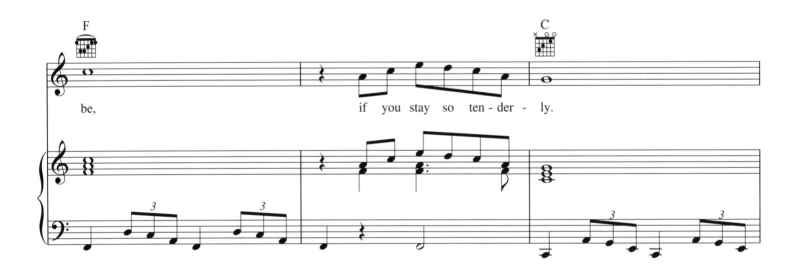

be,   if you stay so ten - der - ly.

Ma - thil - da, I'll cry and cry for you,   yes, no mat - ter what __ you

MY TOOT TOOT

Words and Music by
SIDNEY SIMIEN

Now you can look as much, ___ but if you much as touch, ___
I'm the ac-cor-di-on man ___ from the bay-ou land, ___

you're gon-na have your-self a case.
start-ed the Toot Toot ___ train. ___

I'm gon-na break your face. ___ Don't mess ___ with my
Now I'm the Toot Toot man. ___

Now, don't you mess with my Toot Toot, don't mess ___ with my
Now, don't you mess with my Toot Toot, don't mess ___ with my

D.S. al Coda
(take 2nd ending)

CODA

Don't mess_ with my

F

B♭

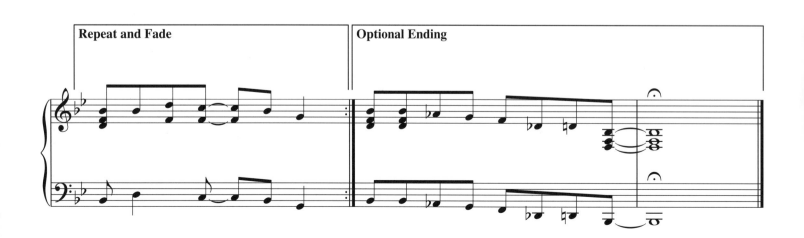

Repeat and Fade

Optional Ending

ORIGINAL NEW JOLE BLON

Words and Music by
HARRY CHOATES

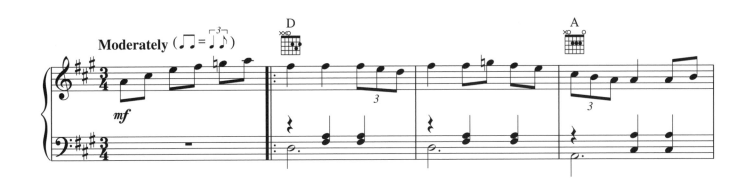

mais mal - eur - euse.
venir mais moi peux a - voir?
dé - fait, pe - tite.

PAPER IN MY SHOE

Words and Music by WILSON "BOOZOO" CHAVIS
and EDDIE SHULER

(1., 3.) I got a pa-per in my shoe, __
(2.) Mo gain pa-pier dans mon sou - lier, __

I got a pa-per in my shoe.
mo gain pa-pier dans mon sou - lier.

Oh, what your ma-ma don't know __
Oh ça ta ma-ma con-nait

— pas,
and what your pa-pa don't like.
et ça ta pop __ aime pas.

PINE GROVE BLUES

Words and Music by
NATHAN ABSHIRE

Hey, ne-gresse, à-yoù toi e-tais hier au soir, ma ne-gresse? Hey, ne-gresse,

YA YA

Words and Music by MORRIS LEVY
and CLARENCE LEWIS

Moderately

(1., D.S.) Sit - tin' here, la la, wait - in' for my ya ya. _____ Mm. _____

(2.) Ba - by, hur - ry, don't __ keep me wor - ry, uh - huh. Ooh

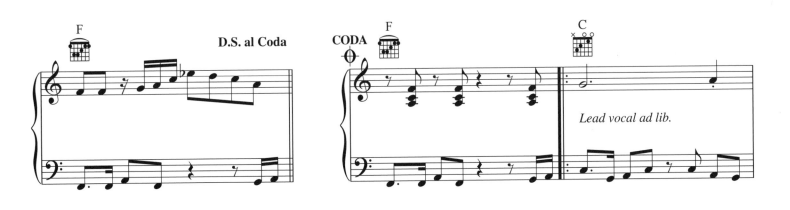

SUGAR BEE

Words and Music by
EDDIE SHULER

said you'd be my hon-ey all night long. When I found you, ba-by, you were
came _ home this morn-in' 'bout a quar-ter to four. Found an-oth-er wom-an sit-tin'

do-in' _ wrong.} Sug-ar Bee, Sug-ar Bee,
at my _ door.}

Sug-ar Bee, Sug-ar

Bee, Sug-ar Bee, Sug-ar Bee, look what _ you done to

To Coda

me. _

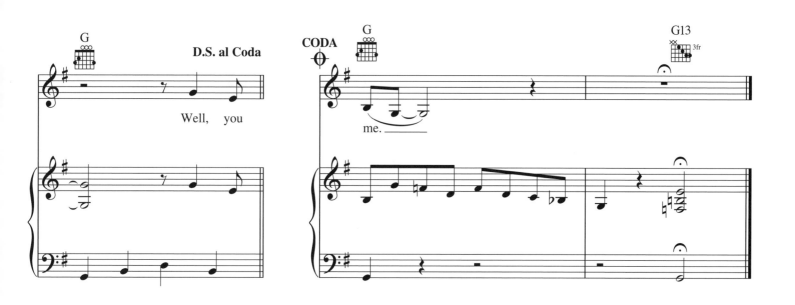

D.S. al Coda

Well,   you

CODA

me.

UNCLE BUD

Words and Music by
WILSON "BOOZOO" CHAVIS

sick in bed.___ Un-cle Bud.
old man moan. _ Un-cle Bud.

1-6 **7**

2. Un-cle

Additional Lyrics

3. Uncle Bud's got cotton ain't never been picked,
   Uncle Bud's got corn ain't never been shucked,
   Uncle Bud's got a daughter ain't never been touched.
   Uncle Bud.

4. Big fish, little fish swimming in the water,
   Some son-of-a-gun done court my daughter.
   Uncle Bud.

5. Down in Louisiana where the grass grow green,
   They've got more women than you ever seen.
   Uncle Bud.

6. Uncle Bud got this, Uncle Bud got that,
   Uncle Bud got a big old cowboy hat.
   Uncle Bud.

7. Yonder come Mark with a pack on his back,
   He bring more cotton than he can pack.
   Uncle Bud.

WHEN THE SAINTS GO MARCHING IN

Words by KATHERINE E. PURVIS
Music by JAMES M. BLACK

Oh, when the saints _____ go march - ing
sun _____ re - fuse to
crown _____ Him Lord of
gath - er 'round the

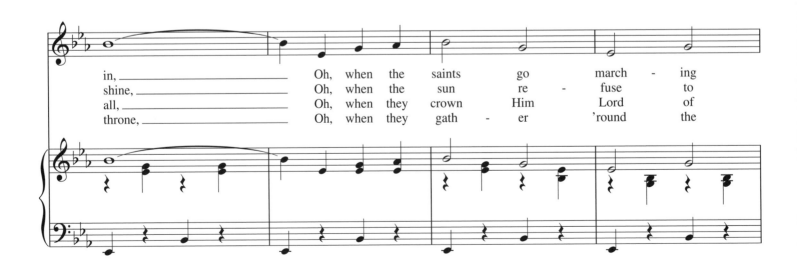

in, _____ Oh, when the saints go march - ing
shine, _____ Oh, when the sun re - fuse to
all, _____ Oh, when they crown Him Lord of
throne, _____ Oh, when they gath - er 'round the

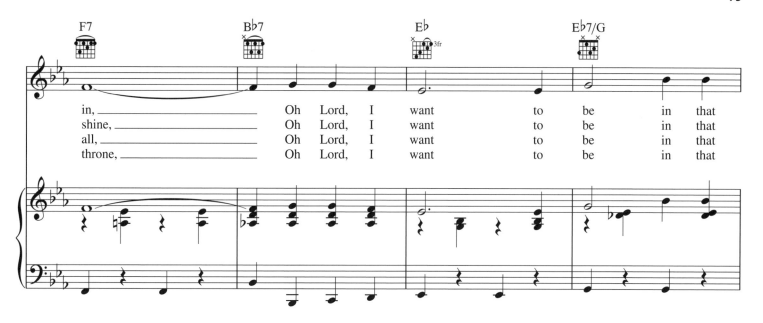

in, _____ Oh Lord, I want to be in that
shine, _____ Oh Lord, I want to be in that
all, _____ Oh Lord, I want to be in that
throne, _____ Oh Lord, I want to be in that

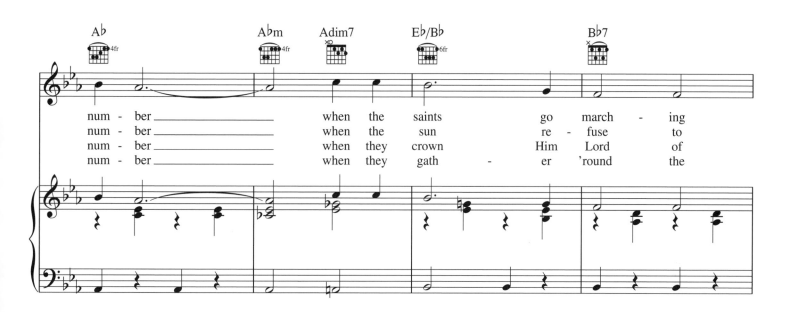

num - ber _____ when the saints go march - ing
num - ber _____ when the sun re - fuse to
num - ber _____ when they crown Him Lord of
num - ber _____ when they gath - er 'round the

in. _____ Oh, when the throne. _____
shine. _____ Oh, when they
all. _____ Oh, when they

YELLOW MOON

Words and Music by AARON NEVILLE
and JOEL NEVILLE

Oh, ___ yel-low moon, ___

___ yel-low moon, ___ why you keep peep-in' in ___ my win-

You can tell me, oh, if the girl's nev-er com-in' back.

Is she

(1.) here out with an-oth-er or is she tryin' to get back home?
(2.) see if she is miss-in' me or is she hav-in' a real good time?

(D.S.) *Sax solo*

Sax solo

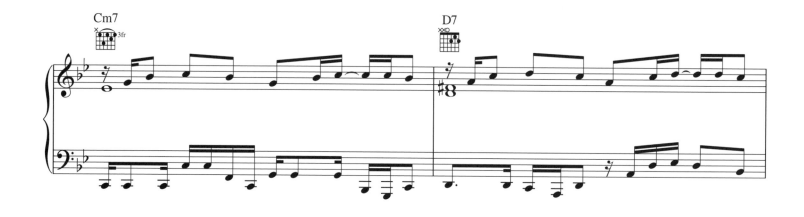

Optional Ending

Repeat and Fade

ZYDECO GRIS GRIS

Words and Music by
MICHAEL DOUCET

Beaux et belles fait ___ ses pro - jects, Ma - man fait grand gris gris. Loin, loin, cy -

- pri - ère noir, tout que-q'un cré - ole crie: Zy - de - co! Zy - de - co!

THE BEST EVER COLLECTION

ARRANGED FOR PIANO, VOICE AND GUITAR

150 of the Most Beautiful Songs Ever
150 ballads: Bewitched • (They Long to Be) Close to You • How Deep Is Your Love • I'll Be Seeing You • Unchained Melody • Yesterday • Young at Heart • more.
00360735 ....$24.95

Best Acoustic Rock Songs Ever
65 acoustic hits: Dust in the Wind • Fast Car • I Will Remember You • Landslide • Leaving on a Jet Plane • Maggie May • Tears in Heaven • Yesterday • more.
00310984 ....$19.95

Best Big Band Songs Ever
Over 60 big band hits: Boogie Woogie Bugle Boy • Don't Get Around Much Anymore • In the Mood • Moonglow • Sentimental Journey • Who's Sorry Now • more.
00359129 ....$16.95

Best Broadway Songs Ever
Over 70 songs in all! Includes: All I Ask of You • Bess, You Is My Woman • Climb Ev'ry Mountain • Comedy Tonight • If I Were a Rich Man • Ol' Man River • more!
00309155 ....$22.95

Best Children's Songs Ever
Over 100 songs: Bingo • Eensy Weensy Spider • The Farmer in the Dell • On Top of Spaghetti • Puff the Magic Dragon • Twinkle, Twinkle Little Star • and more.
00310360 (Easy Piano) $19.95

Best Christmas Songs Ever
More than 60 holiday favorites: Frosty the Snow Man • A Holly Jolly Christmas • I'll Be Home for Christmas • Rudolph, The Red-Nosed Reindeer • Silver Bells • more.
00359130 ....$19.95

Best Classic Rock Songs Ever
Over 60 hits: American Woman • Bang a Gong • Cold As Ice • Heartache Tonight • Rock and Roll All Nite • Smoke on the Water • Wonderful Tonight • and more.
00310800 ....$18.95

Best Classical Songs Ever
Over 80 of classical favorites: Ave Maria • Canon in D • Eine Kleine Nachtmusik • Für Elise • Lacrymosa • Ode to Joy • William Tell Overture • and many more.
00310674 (Piano Solo) $19.95

Best Contemporary Christian Songs Ever
Over 70 favorites, including: Awesome God • El Shaddai • Friends • Jesus Freak • People Need the Lord • Place in This World • Serve the Lord • Thy Word • more.
00310558 ....$19.95

Best Country Songs Ever
78 classic country hits: Always on My Mind • Crazy • Daddy Sang Bass • Forever and Ever, Amen • God Bless the U.S.A. • I Fall to Pieces • Through the Years • more.
00359135 ....$17.95

Best Early Rock 'n' Roll Songs Ever
Over 70 songs, including: Book of Love • Crying • Do Wah Diddy Diddy • Louie, Louie • Peggy Sue • Shout • Splish Splash • Stand By Me • Tequila • and more.
00310816 ....$17.95

Best Easy Listening Songs Ever
75 mellow favorites: (They Long to Be) Close to You • Every Breath You Take • How Am I Supposed to Live Without You • Unchained Melody • more.
00359193 ....$18.95

Best Gospel Songs Ever
80 gospel songs: Amazing Grace • Daddy Sang Bass • How Great Thou Art • I'll Fly Away • Just a Closer Walk with Thee • The Old Rugged Cross • more.
00310503 ....$19.95

Best Hymns Ever
118 hymns: Abide with Me • Every Time I Feel the Spirit • He Leadeth Me • I Love to Tell the Story • Were You There? • When I Survey the Wondrous Cross • and more.
00310774 ....$17.95

Best Jazz Standards Ever
77 jazz hits: April in Paris • Beyond the Sea • Don't Get Around Much Anymore • Misty • Satin Doll • So Nice (Summer Samba) • Unforgettable • and more.
00311641 ....$19.95

More of the Best Jazz Standards Ever
74 beloved jazz hits: Ain't Misbehavin' • Blue Skies • Come Fly with Me • Honeysuckle Rose • The Lady Is a Tramp • Moon River • My Funny Valentine • and more.
00311023 ....$19.95

Best Latin Songs Ever
67 songs: Besame Mucho (Kiss Me Much) • The Girl from Ipanema • Malaguena • Slightly Out of Tune (Desafinado) • Summer Samba (So Nice) • and more.
00310355 ....$19.95

Best Love Songs Ever
65 favorite love songs, including: Endless Love • Here and Now • Love Takes Time • Misty • My Funny Valentine • So in Love • You Needed Me • Your Song.
00359198 ....$19.95

Best Movie Songs Ever
74 songs from the movies: Almost Paradise • Chariots of Fire • My Heart Will Go On • Take My Breath Away • Unchained Melody • You'll Be in My Heart • more.
00310063 ....$19.95

Best Praise & Worship Songs Ever
80 all-time favorites: Awesome God • Breathe • Here I Am to Worship • I Could Sing of Your Love Forever • Open the Eyes of My Heart • Shout to the Lord • more.
00310063 ....$19.95

Best R&B Songs Ever
66 songs, including: Baby Love • Endless Love • Here and Now • I Will Survive • Saving All My Love for You • Stand By Me • What's Going On • and more.
00310184 ....$19.95

Best Rock Songs Ever
Over 60 songs: All Shook Up • Blue Suede Shoes • Born to Be Wild • Every Breath You Take • Free Bird • Hey Jude • We Got the Beat • Wild Thing • more!
00490424 ....$18.95

Best Songs Ever
Over 70 must-own classics: Edelweiss • Love Me Tender • Memory • My Funny Valentine • Tears in Heaven • Unforgettable • A Whole New World • and more.
00359224 ....$22.95

More of the Best Songs Ever
79 more favorites: April in Paris • Candle in the Wind • Endless Love • Misty • My Blue Heaven • My Heart Will Go On • Stella by Starlight • Witchcraft • more.
00310437 ....$19.95

Best Standards Ever, Vol. 1 (A-L)
72 beautiful ballads, including: All the Things You Are • Bewitched • God Bless' the Child • I've Got You Under My Skin • The Lady Is a Tramp • more.
00359231 ....$16.95

More of the Best Standards Ever, Vol. 1 (A-L)
76 all-time favorites: Ain't Misbehavin' • Always • Autumn in New York • Desafinado • Fever • Fly Me to the Moon • Georgia on My Mind • and more.
00310813 ....$17.95

Best Standards Ever, Vol. 2 (M-Z)
72 songs: Makin' Whoopee • Misty • My Funny Valentine • People Will Say We're in Love • Smoke Gets in Your Eyes • Strangers in the Night • Tuxedo Junction • more.
00359232 ....$16.95

More of the Best Standards Ever, Vol. 2 (M-Z)
75 more stunning standards: Mona Lisa • Mood Indigo • Moon River • Norwegian Wood • Route 66 • Sentimental Journey • Stella by Starlight • What'll I Do? • and more.
00310814 ....$17.95

Best Torch Songs Ever
70 sad and sultry favorites: All by Myself • Crazy • Fever • I Will Remember You • Misty • Stormy Weather (Keeps Rainin' All the Time) • Unchained Melody • and more.
00311027 ....$19.95

Best TV Songs Ever
Over 50 fun and catchy theme songs: The Addams Family • The Brady Bunch • Happy Days • Mission: Impossible • Where Everybody Knows Your Name • and more!
00311048 ....$17.95

Best Wedding Songs Ever
70 songs of love and commitment: All I Ask of You • Endless Love • The Lord's Prayer • My Heart Will Go On • Trumpet Voluntary • Wedding March • and more.
00311096 ....$17.95

FOR MORE INFORMATION, SEE YOUR LOCAL MUSIC DEALER, OR WRITE TO:

HAL•LEONARD® CORPORATION
7777 W. BLUEMOUND RD. P.O. BOX 13819 MILWAUKEE, WI 53213

Visit us on-line for complete songlists at
www.halleonard.com

Prices, contents and availability subject to change without notice. Not all products available outside the U.S.A.

0205

Classic Collections Of Your Favorite Songs

arranged for piano, voice, and guitar.

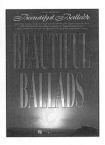

Beautiful Ballads
A massive collection of 87 songs, including: April in Paris • Autumn in New York • Call Me Irresponsible • Cry Me a River • I Wish You Love • I'll Be Seeing You • If • Imagine • Isn't It Romantic? • It's Impossible (Somos Novios) • Mona Lisa • Moon River • People • The Way We Were • A Whole New World (Aladdin's Theme) • and more.
00311679 ....$17.95

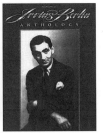

Irving Berlin Anthology
A comprehensive collection of 61 timeless songs with a bio, song background notes, and photos. Songs include: Always • Blue Skies • Cheek to Cheek • God Bless America • Marie • Puttin' on the Ritz • Steppin' Out with My Baby • There's No Business Like Show Business • White Christmas • (I Wonder Why?) You're Just in Love • and more.
00312493 ....$22.95

The Big Book of Standards
86 classics essential to any music library, including: April in Paris • Autumn in New York • Blue Skies • Cheek to Cheek • Heart and Soul • I Left My Heart in San Francisco • In the Mood • Isn't It Romantic? • Mona Lisa • Moon River • The Nearness of You • Out of Nowhere • Spanish Eyes • Star Dust • Stella by Starlight • That Old Black Magic • They Say It's Wonderful • What Now My Love • and more.
00311667 ....$19.95

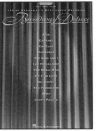

Broadway Deluxe
This exciting collection of 125 of Broadway's biggest show tunes is deluxe indeed! Includes such showstoppers as: Bewitched • Cabaret • Camelot • Day by Day • Hello Young Lovers • I Could Have Danced All Night • I've Grown Accustomed to Her Face • If Ever I Would Leave You • The Lady Is a Tramp • I Talk to the Trees • My Heart Belongs to Daddy • Oklahoma • September Song • Seventy Six Trombones • Try to Remember • and more!
00309245 ....$24.95

Classic Jazz Standards
56 jazz essentials: All the Things You Are • Don't Get Around Much Anymore • How Deep Is the Ocean • In the Wee Small Hours of the Morning • Polka Dots and Moonbeams • Satin Doll • Skylark • Tangerine • Tenderly • What's New? • and more.
00310310 ....$16.95

I'll Be Seeing You: 50 Songs of World War II
A salute to the music and memories of WWII, including a year-by-year chronology of events on the homefront, dozens of photos, and 50 radio favorites of the GIs and their families back home, including: Boogie Woogie Bugle Boy • Don't Sit Under the Apple Tree (With Anyone Else But Me) • I Don't Want to Walk Without You • I'll Be Seeing You • Moonlight in Vermont • There's a Star-Spangled Banner Waving Somewhere • You'd Be So Nice to Come Home To • and more.
00311698 ....$19.95

Lounge Music
Features 45 top requests of the martini crowd: Alfie • Beyond the Sea • Blue Velvet • Call Me Irresponsible • Copacabana • Danke Schoen • Feelings • The Girl from Ipanema • I Will Survive • Mandy • Misty • More • People • That's Life • more.
00310193 ....$14.95

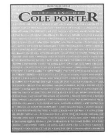

Best of Cole Porter
38 of his classics, including: All of You • Anything Goes • Be a Clown • Don't Fence Me In • I Get a Kick Out of You • In the Still of the Night • Let's Do It (Let's Fall in Love) • Night and Day • You Do Something to Me • and many more.
00311577 ....$14.95

Big Band Favorites
A great collection of 70 of the best Swing Era songs, including: East of the Sun • Honeysuckle Rose • I Can't Get Started with You • I'll Be Seeing You • In the Mood • Let's Get Away from It All • Moonglow • Moonlight in Vermont • Opus One • Stompin' at the Savoy • Tuxedo Junction • more!
00310445 ....$16.95

The Best of Rodgers & Hammerstein
A capsule of 26 classics from this legendary duo. Songs include: Climb Ev'ry Mountain • Edelweiss • Getting to Know You • I'm Gonna Wash That Man Right Outta My Hair • My Favorite Things • Oklahoma • The Surrey with the Fringe on Top • You'll Never Walk Alone • and more.
00308210 ....$16.95

The Best Songs Ever – 5th Edition
Over 70 must-own classics, including: All I Ask of You • Body and Soul • Crazy • Fly Me to the Moon • Here's That Rainy Day • Imagine • Love Me Tender • Memory • Moonlight in Vermont • My Funny Valentine • People • Satin Doll • Save the Best for Last • Tears in Heaven • A Time for Us • The Way We Were • What a Wonderful World • When I Fall in Love • and more.
00359224 .... $22.95

Torch Songs
Sing your heart out with this collection of 59 sultry jazz and big band melancholy masterpieces, including: Angel Eyes • Cry Me a River • I Can't Get Started • I Got It Bad and That Ain't Good • I'm Glad There Is You • Lover Man (Oh, Where Can You Be?) • Misty • My Funny Valentine • Stormy Weather • and many more! 224 pages.
00490446 ....$17.95

0204